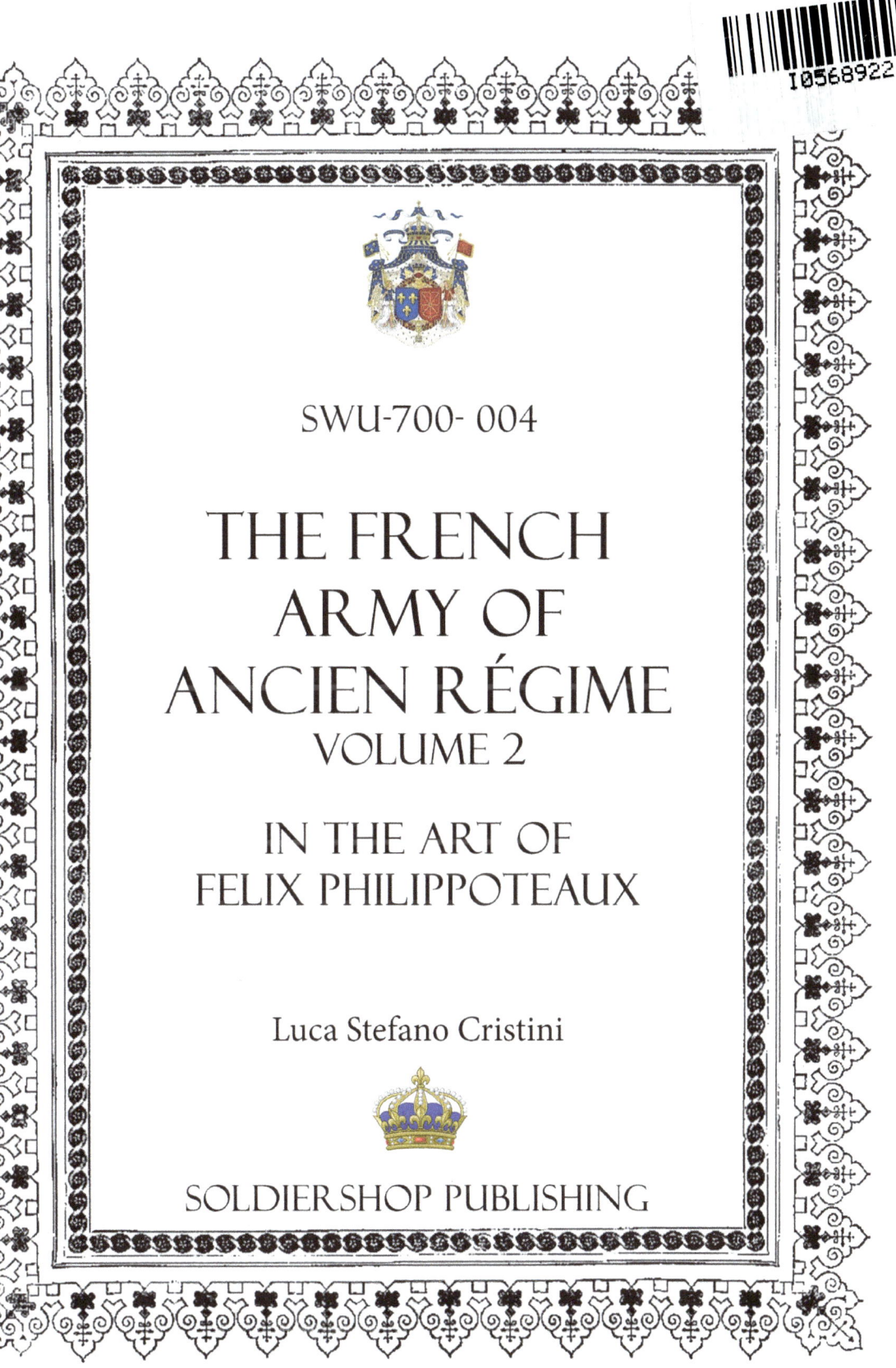

SWU-700- 004

THE FRENCH ARMY OF ANCIEN RÉGIME
VOLUME 2

IN THE ART OF FELIX PHILIPPOTEAUX

Luca Stefano Cristini

SOLDIERSHOP PUBLISHING

AUTHOR

Henri Félix Emmanuel Philippoteaux (1815-1884) was a French artist. He was born in Paris, France, studied art at the studio of Leon Cogniet, and first exhibited his work at the Paris Salon of 1833. One of his most well-known works was a depiction of the Siege of Paris during the Franco-Prussian War, painted in the form of a cyclorama.

Title: **The French army of ancien Régime VOL. 2 - In the art of Felix Philippoteaux**
By Luca Stefano Cristini. Plates of F. Philippoteaux. First edition September 2016 by Soldiershop. Cover & Art Design: Luca S. Cristini. ISBN code: 978-88-93271202

Published by Soldiershop publishing, via Padre Davide, 7 - 24050 Zanica (BG) ITALY. www.soldiershop.com

THE FRENCH ARMY
OF ANCIEN RÉGIME
VOLUME 2

*

IN THE ART OF
FELIX PHILIPPOTEAUX

HISTORICAL ILLUSTRATIONS OF THE CLOTHING AND ARMS
OF THE FRENCH ARMY BY FELIX PHILIPPOTEAUX

Henri Félix Emmanuel Philippoteaux (1815-1884) was a French artist. He was born in Paris, France, studied art at the studio of Leon Cogniet, and first exhibited his work at the Paris Salon of 1833. One of his most well-known works was a depiction of the Siege of Paris during the Franco-Prussian War, painted in the form of a cyclorama, a type of large panoramic painting on the inside of a cylindrical platform designed to provide a viewer standing in the middle of the cylinder with a 360° view of the painting.

Viewers surrounded by the panoramic image are meant to feel as if they are standing in the midst of a historic event or famous place.

Philippoteaux also produced a large number of works chronicling the rise and successes of Napoleon Bonaparte, including a portrait of Napoleon in his regimental uniform and a group of paintings of French victories in the Napoleonic Wars. Philippoteaux was awarded the Légion d'honneur in 1846.

Philippoteaux's son Paul Philippoteaux was also an artist; both were famous for their production of cycloramas. Father and son collaborated on The Defence of the Fort d'Issy in 1871. They also collaborated on a cyclorama of the Battle of Gettysburg that became a celebrated work in the United States: *"One cyclorama, however, halted the slide in popularity, and almost single-handedly revived the public's interest in the medium for another decade...this singular creation was initially painted in 1882-83 by Henry F. Philippoteaux and Paul Philippoteaux, a father and son team of French artists...within a year, half a million people had stood before it."*

Father and son enhanced the artistic effect of their cylindrical painting by adding a third dimension, including elements of diorama placed in front of the painting, and by incorporating sections of walls and battlefield objects that blended into the painted parts of the presentation. He died in 1884 and his obituary in the New York Times appeared on November 10, 1884.

This book, utilize several plates of an our copy of the book *"Atlas de l'Histoire de l'ancienne infanterie française"* Paris, J. Corréard, 1853. All the images has been restored by human beings, page by page, so that you may enjoy it in a form as close to the original as possible. Our work it is realized on two volume.

◄ *Louis XIV King of France painted by Hyacinthe Rigaud (1659-1743)*

CONTENTS

*

LOUIS XIV KING OF FRANCE

Louis XIV (5 September 1638 – 1 September 1715), known as Louis the Great (Louis le Grand) or the Sun King (*le Roi-Soleil*), was the great a monarch who ruled as King of France from 1643 until his death in 1715. His reign of 72 years and 110 days is the longest of any monarch of a major country in European history. In this age of absolutism in Europe, well know ad *Ancien regime*, Louis XIV's France was a leader in the growing centralization of power.

Louis began his personal rule of France in 1661 after the death of his chief minister, the Italian Cardinal Mazarin. An adherent of the concept of the divine right of kings, which advocates the divine origin of monarchical rule, Louis continued his predecessors' work of creating a centralized state governed from the capital. He sought to eliminate the remnants of feudalism persisting in parts of France and, by compelling many members of the nobility to inhabit his lavish Palace of Versailles (formerly a hunting lodge belonging to Louis's father), succeeded in pacifying the aristocracy, many members of which had participated in the Fronde rebellion during Louis's minority. By these means he became one of the most powerful French monarchs and consolidated a system of absolute monarchical rule in France that endured until the French Revolution.

During Louis's reign, France was the leading European power and it fought three major wars: the Franco-Dutch War, the War of the League of Augsburg, and the War of the Spanish Succession. There were also two lesser conflicts: the War of Devolution and the War of the Reunions. Louis encouraged and benefited from the work of prominent political, military, and cultural figures such as Mazarin, Colbert, the Grand Condé, Turenne and Vauban, as well as Molière, Racine, Boileau, La Fontaine, Lully, Marais, Le Brun, Rigaud, Bossuet, Le Vau, Mansart, Charles and Claude Perrault, and Le Nôtre. Upon his death just days before his 77th birthday, Louis was succeeded by his five-year-old great-grandson, Louis XV. All of his intermediate heirs predeceased him: his son Louis, le Grand Dauphin; the Dauphin's eldest son Louis, Duke of Burgundy; and Burgundy's eldest son Louis, Duke of Brittany (the elder brother of Louis XV).

EARLY YEARS

Louis XIV was born on 5 September 1638 in the Château de Saint-Germain-en-Laye to Louis XIII and Anne of Austria. He was named Louis Dieudonné (Louis the God-given) and also bore the traditional title of French heirs apparent: Dauphin. At the time of his birth, his parents had been married for 23 years. His mother had experienced four stillbirths between 1619 and 1631. Leading contemporaries thus regarded him as a divine gift, and his birth a miracle of God. Sensing imminent death, Louis XIII decided to put his affairs in order in the spring of 1643, when Louis XIV was four years old. In defiance of custom, which would have made Queen Anne the sole Regent of France, he decreed that a regency council would rule on his son's behalf. His lack of faith in Queen Anne's political abilities was the primary reason. He did, however, make the concession of appointing her head of the council. Louis's relationship with his mother was uncommonly affectionate for the time. Contemporaries and eyewitnesses claimed that the Queen would spend all her time with Louis. Both were greatly interested in food and theatre, and it is highly likely that Louis developed these interests through his close relationship with his mother. This long-lasting and loving relationship can be evidenced by excerpts in Louis's journal entries: *"Nature was responsible for the first knots which tied me to my mother. But attachments formed later by shared qualities of the spirit are far more difficult to break than those formed merely by blood."* It was his mother who gave Louis his belief in the absolute and divine power of his monarchical rule. In 1646 Nicolas V de Villeroy became the young king's tutor. Louis XIV became friends with his young children, particularly François de Villeroy, and divided his time between the Palais-Royal and the nearby Hotel de Villeroy Minority and the *Fronde*.

ACCESSION

On 13 May 1643, with Louis XIII dead, Queen Anne had her husband's will annulled by the Parlement de Paris (a judicial body comprising mostly nobles and high clergymen). This action abolished the regency council and made Anne sole Regent of France. Anne exiled some of her husband's ministers (Chavigny, Bouthilier) and she nominated Brienne as her minister of foreign affairs; she also nominated Saint Vincent de Paul as her spiritual advisor which helped her deal with religious policy and the Jansenism question. Anne kept the direction of religious policy strongly in her hand until 1661; her most important political decisions were to nominate Cardinal Mazarin as her chief minister and her decision to continue her husband's and Richelieu's policy, in spite of their persecution of her, for the sake of her son. Anne wanted to give her son an absolute authority and a victorious kingdom.

Her choice of Mazarin was mainly because of his ability and his total dependence on her at least until 1653 when she was no longer regent. Anne protected Mazarin by arresting and exiling her followers who conspired against him in 1643: the Duke of Beaufort and Marie de Rohan. She left the direction of the daily administration of policy to Cardinal Mazarin. The best example of Anne's statesmanship and the partial change in her heart towards her native Spain, is seen in her keeping of one of Richelieu's men the chancellor of France Pierre Séguier in his post.

Séguier was the person who interrogated Anne in 1637, treating her like a "*common criminal*" as she herself described her treatment following the discovery that she was giving military secrets and information to Spain.

Anne was virtually under house arrest for a number of years during her husband's rule and was physically searched and almost insulted by the chancellor according to certain sources. By keeping him in his post, Anne was giving a sign that the interests of France and her son Louis were the guiding spirit of all her political and legal actions.

Though not necessarily opposed to Spain, she sought to end the war with a French victory in order to establish a lasting peace between the Catholic nations; the queen also gave a partial Catholic orientation to France foreign policy which was felt by the Netherlands, the Protestant ally of France, which negotiated a separate peace with Spain in 1648. In 1648, Anne and Mazarin successfully negotiated the Peace of Westphalia, which ended the Thirty Years' War in Germany. Its terms ensured Dutch independence from Spain, awarded some autonomy to the various German princes of the Holy Roman Empire, and granted Sweden seats on the Imperial Diet and territories to control the mouths of the Oder, Elbe, and Weser rivers. France, however, profited most from the settlement.

Austria, ruled by the Habsburg Emperor Ferdinand III, ceded all Habsburg lands and claims in Alsace to France and acknowledged her de facto sovereignty over the Three Bishoprics of Metz, Verdun, and Toul. Moreover, eager to emancipate themselves from Habsburg domination, petty German states sought French protection. This anticipated the formation of the 1658 League of the Rhine, leading to the further diminution of Imperial power.

EARLY ACTS

As the Thirty Years' War came to an end, a civil war known as the Fronde (after the slings used to smash windows) erupted in France. It effectively checked France's ability to exploit the Peace of Westphalia. Anne and Mazarin had largely pursued the policies of Cardinal Richelieu, augmenting the Crown's power at the expense of the nobility and the Parlements. Anne interfered much more in internal policy than foreign affairs; she was a very proud queen who insisted on the divine rights of the king of France. All this led her to advocate a forceful policy in all matters relating to the king's authority in a manner that was much more radical than the one proposed by Mazarin.

The Cardinal depended totally on Anne support and had to use all his influence on the queen in order not to nullify but to restrain some of her radical actions. Anne imprisoned any aristocrat or member of parliament who challenged her will; her main aim was to transfer to her son an absolute authority in the matters of finance and justice.

She went as far as jailing leaders of the Parlement of Paris and one of them even died in prison. The Frondeurs, political heirs of a dissatisfied feudal aristocracy, sought to protect their traditional feudal privileges from an increasingly centralized royal government. Furthermore, they believed their traditional influence and authority was being usurped by the recently ennobled bureaucrats (*the Noblesse de Robe*, or "nobility of the robe") who administered the kingdom and on whom the monarchy increasingly began to rely. This belief intensified their resentment. In 1648 Anne and Mazarin attempted to tax members of the Parlement de Paris.

The members not only refused to comply, but also ordered all of his earlier financial edicts burned. Buoyed by the victory of Louis, duc d'Enghien (later known as le Grand Condé) at the Battle of Lens, Mazarin, on Queen Anne's insistence, arrested certain members in a show of force. The most important arrest from Anne's point of view concerned Pierre Broussel, one of the most important leaders in the Parlement de Paris. People in France were complaining about the expansion of royal authority, the high rate of taxation and the reduction of the authority of *"the Parlement de Paris"* and other regional representatives entities. Paris erupted in rioting as a result and Anne was forced under intense pressure to liberate Broussel. A mob of angry Parisians broke into the royal palace and demanded to see their king. Led into the royal bedchamber, they gazed upon Louis, who was feigning sleep, were appeased, and quietly departed. The threat to the royal family prompted Anne to flee Paris with the king and his courtiers. Shortly thereafter, the conclusion of the Peace of Westphalia allowed Condé's army to return to aid Louis and his court. Condé's family was close to Anne at that period of time and he agreed to help her in her attempt to restore the king's authority. The queen's army, headed by Condé, attacked the rebels in Paris,; the rebels were under the political control of Anne's old friend Marie de Rohan. Beaufort who escaped from the prison where Anne imprisoned him 5 years before, was the military leader in Paris under the nominal control of Conti. After a few battles a political compromise was reached; the Peace of Rueil was signed and the court returned to Paris. Unfortunately for Anne, her partial victory depended on Conde who wanted to control the queen and to destroy the influence of Mazarin. It was Conde's sister who pushed him to turn against the queen. After striking a deal with her old friend Marie de Rohan who was able to impose the nomination of Charles de l'Aubespine, marquis de Châteauneuf as minister of justice; Anne arrested Conde, his brother Armand de Bourbon, Prince of Conti and the husband of their sister Anne Genevieve de Bourbon, duchess of Longueville. This situation did not last very long and the unpopularity of Mazarin led to the creation of a coalition who was headed mainly by Marie de Rohan and the duchess of Longueville. This aristocratic coalition was strong enough to liberate the princes, exile Mazarin and to impose a condition of virtual house arrest on Queen Anne. All these events

▲ *Louis XIV of France and his family. Canvas attributed to Nicolas de Largillière.*

would be witnessed by Louis and would largely explain his later distrust of Paris and the higher aristocracy *"In one sense, Louis' childhood came to an end with the outbreak of the Fronde. It was not only that life became insecure and unpleasant – a fate meted out to many children in all ages – but that Louis had to be taken into the confidence of his mother and Mazarin and political and military matters of which he could have no deep understanding"*. *"The family home became at times a near-prison when Paris had to be abandoned, not in carefree outings to other chateaux but in humiliating flights"*. The royal family was driven out of Paris twice in this manner, and at one point Louis XIV and Anne were held under virtual arrest in the royal palace in Paris. The Fronde years planted in Louis a hatred of Paris and a consequent determination to move out of the ancient capital as soon as possible, never to return. Just as the first Fronde (the Fronde parlementaire of 1648–1649) ended, a second one (the Fronde des princes of 1650–1653) began. Unlike that which preceded it, tales of sordid intrigue and half-hearted warfare characterized this second phase of upper-class insurrection. To the aristocracy, this rebellion represented a protest against and a reversal of their political demotion from vassals to courtiers.

It was headed by the highest-ranking French nobles, among them Louis's uncle Gaston, Duke of Orléans,

▲ *A satire sheet about the conditions of the third Estate.*

and first cousin Anne Marie Louise d'Orléans, Duchess of Montpensier, known as la Grande Mademoiselle; Princes of the Blood such as Condé, his brother Armand, Prince of Conti, and their sister the Duchess of Longueville; dukes of legitimised royal descent, such as Henri, Duke of Longueville, and François, Duke of Beaufort; so-called *"foreign princes"* such as Frédéric Maurice, Duke of Bouillon, his brother Marshal Turenne, and Marie de Rohan, Duchess of Chevreuse; and scions of France's oldest families, such as François de La Rochefoucauld. Queen Anne played the most important role in defeating the Fronde because she wanted to transfer absolute authority to her son. In addition, most of the princes refused to deal with Mazarin, who went into exile for a number of years. The Frondeurs claimed to act on Louis's behalf and in his real interest against his mother and Mazarin. Queen Anne had a very close relationship with the Cardinal, and many observers believed that Mazarin became Louis XIV's stepfather by a secret marriage to Queen Anne. However, Louis's coming-of-age and subsequent coronation deprived them of the Frondeurs' pretext for revolt. The Fronde thus gradually lost steam and ended in 1653, when Mazarin returned triumphantly from exile. From that time till his death, Mazarin was in charge of foreign and financial policy without the daily supervision of Anne, who was no longer regent. During this period, Louis fell in love with Mazarin's niece Marie Mancini, but Anne and Mazarin ended the king's infatuation by sending Mancini away from court to be married in Italy. While Mazarin might have been tempted for a short period of time to marry his niece to the King of France, Queen Anne was absolutely against this; she wanted to marry her son to the daughter of her brother, Philip IV of Spain, for both dynastic and political reasons.

Mazarin soon supported the Queen's position because he knew that her support for his power and his foreign policy depended on making peace with Spain from a strong position and on the Spanish marriage. In addition, Mazarin's relations with Marie Mancini were not good and he did not trust her to support his position. All of Louis' tears and his supplications to his mother did not make her change her mind; the Spanish marriage was very important not only for its role in ending the war between France and Spain but also in the fact that much of the claims and objectives of Louis' foreign policy in the next 50 years would be based on this marriage.

PERSONAL REIGN AND REFORMS

Coming of age and early reforms

Louis XIV was declared to have reached the age of majority in 1654. On the death of Mazarin in March 1661, Louis assumed personal control of the reins of government and astonished his court by declaring that he would rule without a chief minister: *"Up to this moment I have been pleased to entrust the government of my affairs to the late Cardinal. It is now time that I govern them myself. You (he was talking to the secretaries and ministers of state) will assist me with your counsels when I ask for them. I request and order you to seal no orders except by my command . . . I order you not to sign anything, not even a passport . . . without my command; to render account to me personally each day and to favor no one"*. Louis was able to capitalize on the widespread public yearning for law and order that resulted from prolonged foreign wars and domestic civil strife to further consolidate central political authority and reform at the expense of the feudal aristocracy. Praising his ability to choose and encourage men of talent, the historian Chateaubriand noted that *"it is the voice of genius of all kinds which sounds from the tomb of Louis"*.

Louis began his personal reign with administrative and fiscal reforms. In 1661, the treasury verged on bankruptcy. To rectify the situation, Louis chose Jean-Baptiste Colbert as Controller-General of Finances in 1665. However, Louis first had to neutralize Nicolas Fouquet, the Superintendent of Finances, in order to give Colbert a free hand.

Although Fouquet's financial indiscretions were not really very different from Mazarin before him or Colbert after him, his ambition was worrying to Louis. He had, for example, built an opulent château at Vaux-le-Vicomte where he entertained Louis and his court ostentatiously, as if he were wealthier than the king himself. The court was left with the impression that the vast sums of money needed to support his lifestyle could only have been obtained through embezzlement of government funds. Fouquet appeared eager to succeed Mazarin and Richelieu in assuming power, and he indiscreetly purchased and privately fortified the remote island of Belle Île. These acts sealed his doom. Fouquet was charged with embezzlement. The Parlement found him guilty and sentenced him to exile. However, Louis altered the sentence to life-imprisonment and abolished Fouquet's post.

With Fouquet dismissed, Colbert reduced the national debt through more efficient taxation. The principal taxes included the aides and douanes (both customs duties), the gabelle (a tax on salt), and the taille (a tax on land).

The taille was reduced at first, financial officials were forced to keep regular accounts, auctioning certain taxes instead of selling them privately to a favored few, revising inventories and removing unauthorized exemptions (for example in 1661 only 10 per cent from the royal domain reached the King).

Reform proved difficult because the taille was levied by officers of the Crown who had purchased their post at a high price: punishment of abuses necessarily lowered the value of the post. Nevertheless, excellent results were achieved, the deficit of 1661 turned into a surplus in 1666. The interest of the debt was reduced from 52 millions to 24 millions livres. The taille was reduced to 42 millions in 1661 and 35 millions in 1665; finally the revenue from indirect taxation progressed from 26 millions to 55 millions. The revenues of the royal domain were raised from 80,000 livres in 1661 to 5,5 million livres in 1671. In 1661 the receipts were equivalent to 26 millions British pounds of which 10 millions reached the treasury. The expenditure was around 18 million pounds leaving a deficit of 8 million. In 1667 the net receipts had risen to 20 million pounds sterling while expenditure had fallen to 11 millions leaving a surplus of 9 million pounds. To support the reorganized and enlarged army, the panoply of Versailles, and the growing civil administration, the king needed a good deal of money. Finance was always the weak spot in the French monarchy. Methods of collecting taxes were costly and inefficient. Direct taxes passed through the hands of many intermediate officials; indirect taxes were collected by private concessionaries called tax farmers who made a substantial profit. The state always received far less than what the taxpayers actually paid. But the main weakness arose from an old bargain between the French crown and nobility; the king might raise without consent if only he refrained from taxing the nobles. Only the *"unprivileged"* classes paid direct taxes, and these came to mean the peasants only, since many bourgeois in one way or others obtained exemptions. The system was outrageously unjust in throwing a heavy tax burden on the poor and helpless. Later after 1700, the French ministers who were supported by Madame De Maintenon were able to convince the King to change his fiscal policy. Louis was willing enough to tax the nobles but was unwilling to fall under their control, and only towards the close of his reign, under extreme stress of war, was he able, for the first time in French History, to impose direct taxes on the aristocratic elements of the population. This was a step toward equality before the law and toward sound public finance, but so many concessions and exemptions were won by nobles and bourgeois that the reform lost much of its value.

Louis and Colbert also had wide-ranging plans to bolster French commerce and trade. Colbert's mercantilist administration established new industries and encouraged manufacturers and inventors, such as the Lyon silk manufacturers and the Gobelins manufactory, a producer of tapestries. He invited manufacturers and artisans from all over Europe to France, such as Murano glassmakers, Swedish ironworkers, and Dutch shipbuilders. In this way, he aimed to decrease foreign imports while increasing French exports, hence reducing the net outflow of precious metals from France.

Louis instituted reforms in military administration through Michel le Tellier and his son François-Michel le Tellier, Marquis de Louvois. They helped to curb the independent spirit of the nobility, imposing order on them at court and in the army. Gone were the days when generals protracted war at the frontiers while bickering over precedence and ignoring orders from the capital and the larger politico-diplomatic picture. The old military aristocracy (*the Noblesse d'épée*, or "nobility of the sword") ceased to have a monopoly over senior military positions and rank. Louvois in particular pledged himself to modernizing the army and re-organizing it into a professional, disciplined and well-trained force. He was devoted to the soldiers' material well-being and morale, and even tried to direct campaigns.

RELATIONS WITH THE MAJOR COLONIES

Legal matters did not escape Louis's attention, as is reflected in the numerous *"Great Ordinances"* he enacted. Pre-revolutionary France was a patchwork of legal systems, with as many legal customs as there were provinces, and two co-existing legal traditions—customary law in the north and Roman civil law in the south.

The 'Grande Ordonnance de Procédure Civile' of 1667, also known as the Code Louis, was a comprehensive legal code attempting a uniform regulation of civil procedure throughout legally irregular France. Among other things, it prescribed baptismal, marriage, and death records in the state's registers, not the church's, and also strictly regulated the right of the Parlements to remonstrate. The Code Louis played an important part in French legal history as the basis for the Napoleonic code, itself the origin of many modern legal codes. One of Louis's more infamous decrees was the Grande Ordonnance sur les Colonies of 1685, also known as the Code Noir *("black code")*. Although it sanctioned slavery, it did attempt to humanise the practice by prohibiting the separation of families. Additionally, in the colonies, only Roman Catholics could own slaves, and these had to be baptised. Louis ruled through a number of councils: *Conseil d'en haut* ("High Council", concerning the most important matters of state)- composed of the king, the crown prince, the minister of finance or the controleur general des finances and finally the secretaries of state in charge of various departments. The members of that council were called ministers of state. *Conseil des depeches* ("Council of Messages", concerning notices and administrative reports from the provinces). *Conseil de Conscience* ("Council of Conscience", concerning religious affairs and episcopal appointments). *Conseil royal des finances* ("Royal Council of Finances") who was headed by the "chef du conseil des finances" (an honorary post in most cases), one of the few posts in the council who where opened to the high aristocracy.

EARLY WARS IN THE LOW COUNTRIES
Spain

The death of King Philip IV of Spain in 1665 precipitated the War of Devolution. In 1660 Louis married Philip IV's eldest daughter, Maria Theresa, as one of the provisions of the 1659 Treaty of the Pyrenees.

The marriage treaty specified that Maria Theresa was to renounce all claims to Spanish territory for herself and all her descendants. Mazarin and Lionne, however, made the renunciation conditional on the full payment of a Spanish dowry of 500,000 écus. The dowry was never paid and would later play a part persuading Charles II of Spain to leave his empire to Philip, Duke of Anjou (later Philip V of Spain), the grandson of Louis and Maria Theresa.

The War of Devolution did not focus on the payment of the dowry. Rather, Louis's pretext for war was the *"devolution"* of land. In Brabant, children of first marriages traditionally were not disadvantaged by their parents' remarriages and still inherited property. Louis's wife was Philip IV's daughter by his first marriage, while the new King of Spain, Charles II, was his son by a subsequent marriage. Thus, Brabant allegedly *"devolved"* on Maria Theresa. This excuse led to France's attack on the Spanish Netherlands.

RELATIONS WITH THE DUTCH

Internal problems in the Dutch Republic aided Louis's designs. The most prominent politician in the Dutch Republic at the time, the *"Grand Pensionary"* Johan de Witt, feared the ambition of the young William III, Prince of Orange, specifically dispossession of his supreme power and the restoration of the House of Orange to the influence it had enjoyed before the death of William II, Prince of Orange. The Dutch were thus initially more preoccupied with domestic affairs than the French advance into Spanish territory. Moreover, the French were nominally their allies against the English in the ongoing Second Anglo-Dutch War. Shocked by the rapidity of French successes and fearful of the future, the Dutch decided to abandon their nominal allies and made peace with England. Joined by Sweden, the English and Dutch formed a Triple Alliance in 1668.

The threat of an escalation of the conflict in the Low Countries and a secret treaty partitioning the Spanish succession with Holy Roman Emperor Leopold I, the other major claimant to the throne of Spain, induced Louis to make peace. The Triple Alliance did not last very long. In 1670 French gold bought the adherence of Charles II of England to the secret Treaty of Dover. France and England, along with certain Rhineland princes, declared war on the Dutch Republic in 1672, igniting the Franco-Dutch War. The rapid invasion and occupation of most of the Netherlands precipitated a coup that toppled De Witt and brought William III to power. In 1674, when France lost the assistance of England, which sued for peace by the Treaty of Westminster, William III received the help of Spain, the Emperor Leopold I, and the rest of the Holy Roman Empire. Despite these diplomatic reversals, the French continued to triumph against overwhelming opposing forces.

Within a few weeks, French forces led by Louis captured all of the Spanish-held Franche-Comté in 1674. Despite being greatly outnumbered, Condé trounced William III's coalition army of Austrians, Spaniards, and Dutchmen at the Battle of Seneffe, and prevented him from descending on Paris. Another outnumbered general, Turenne, conducted a daring and brilliant campaign in the winter of 1674–1675 against the Imperial armies under Raimondo Montecuccoli, driving them back across the Rhine river out of Alsace, which had been invaded.

Through a series of feints, marches, and counter-marches in 1678, Louis besieged and captured Ghent. By placing Louis in a military position far superior to his enemies, these victories brought the war to a speedy end. Six years of war had exhausted Europe, and peace negotiations were soon concluded in 1678 with the Treaty of Nijmegen. Although Louis returned all Dutch territory he captured, he retained the Franche-Comté and gained more land in the Spanish Netherlands. The conclusion of a general peace permitted Louis to intervene in the Scanian War in 1679 on behalf of his ally Sweden. He forced Brandenburg-Prussia to the peace table at the Treaty of Saint-Germain-en-Laye and imposed peace on Denmark-Norway by the Treaty of Fontainebleau and the Peace of Lund, all concluded in 1679. The successful conclusion of the Treaty of Nijmegen enhanced French influence in Europe, but Louis was still not satisfied. In 1679 he dismissed his foreign minister Simon Arnauld, marquis de Pomponne, because he was seen as having compromised too much with the allies. Louis maintained the strength of his army, but in his next series of territorial claims, Louis avoided using military force alone. Rather, he combined it with legal pretexts in his efforts to augment the boundaries of his kingdom. Contemporary treaties were intentionally phrased ambiguously.

Louis established the Chambers of Reunion to determine the full extent of his rights and obligations under those treaties. Cities and territories such as Luxembourg and Casale were prized for their strategic position on the frontier and access to important waterways. Louis also sought Strasbourg, an important strategic crossing on the left bank of the Rhine and heretofore a Free Imperial City of the Holy Roman Empire, annexing it and other territories in 1681.

Although a part of Alsace, Strasbourg was not part of Habsburg-ruled Alsace and was thus not ceded to France in the Peace of Westphalia. Following these annexations, Spain declared war, precipitating the War of the Reunions. However, the Spanish were rapidly defeated because the Emperor (distracted by the Great Turkish War) abandoned them, and the Dutch only supported them minimally. By the Truce of Ratisbon in 1684, Spain was forced to acquiesce in French occupation of most of the conquered territories for 20 years. Louis's policy of the Réunions may have raised France to its greatest size and power during his reign, but it alienated much of Europe. This poor public opinion was compounded by French actions off the Barbary Coast and at Genoa. First, Louis had Algiers and Tripoli, two Barbary pirate strongholds, bombarded to obtain a favourable treaty and the liberation of Christian slaves. Next, in 1684, a punitive mission was launched against Genoa in retaliation for its support for Spain in previous wars.

Although the Genoese submitted and the Doge led an official mission of apology to Versailles, France gained a reputation for brutality and arrogance. European apprehension at growing French might and the realisation of the extent of the dragonnades' effect (discussed below) led many states to abandon their alliance with France. Accordingly, by the late 1680s, France became increasingly isolated in Europe.

NON-EUROPEAN RELATIONS AND THE COLONIES

French colonies multiplied in the Americas, Asia, and Africa during Louis's reign, and French explorers made important discoveries in North America. Louis Jolliet and Jacques Marquette discovered the Mississippi River in 1673. In 1682, René-Robert Cavelier, Sieur de La Salle, followed the Mississippi to the Gulf of Mexico and claimed the vast Mississippi basin in Louis's name, calling it Louisiane. French trading posts were also established in India at Chandernagore and Pondicherry, and in the Indian Ocean at Île Bourbon. Meanwhile, diplomatic relations were initiated with distant countries. In 1669, Suleiman Aga led an Ottoman embassy to revive the old Franco-Ottoman alliance. Then, in 1682, after the reception of the Moroccan embassy of Mohammed Tenim in France, Moulay Ismail, Sultan of Morocco, allowed French consular and commercial establishments in his country. Louis once again received a Moroccan ambassador, Abdallah bin Aisha, in 1699. He also received a Persian embassy led by Mohammad Reza Beg in 1715. From farther afield, Siam dispatched an embassy in 1684, reciprocated by the French magnificently the next year under Alexandre, Chevalier de Chaumont.

This, in turn, was succeeded by another Siamese embassy under Kosa Pan superbly received at Versailles in 1686. Louis then sent another embassy in 1687 under Simon de la Loubère, and French influence grew at the Siamese court, which granted Mergui as a naval base to France. However, the death of Narai, King of Ayutthaya, the execution of his pro-French minister Constantine Phaulkon and the Siege of Bangkok in 1688 ended this era of French influence. France also attempted to participate actively in Jesuit missions to China. To break the Portuguese dominance there, Louis sent Jesuit missionaries to the court of the Kangxi Emperor in 1685: Jean de Fontaney, Joachim Bouvet, Jean-François Gerbillon, Louis Le Comte, and Claude de Visdelou). Louis also received a Chinese Jesuit, Michael Shen Fu-Tsung, at Versailles in 1684. Furthermore, Louis's librarian and translator Arcadio Huang was Chinese.

HEIGHT OF POWER
Centralisation of power

By the early 1680s Louis had greatly augmented French influence in the world. Domestically, he successfully increased the influence of the crown and its authority over the church and aristocracy, thus consolidating absolute monarchy in France. Louis initially supported traditional Gallicanism, which limited papal authority in France, and convened an Assembly of the French clergy in November 1681. Before its dissolution eight months later, the Assembly had accepted the Declaration of the Clergy of France, which increased royal authority at the expense of papal power. Without royal approval, bishops could not leave France and appeals could not be made to the Pope. Additionally, government officials could not be excommunicated for acts committed in pursuance of their duties. Although the king could not make ecclesiastical law, all papal regulations without royal assent were invalid in France. Unsurprisingly, the pope repudiated the Declaration. By attaching nobles to his court at Versailles, Louis achieved increased control over the French aristocracy. Apartments were built to house those willing to pay court to the king. However, the pensions and privileges necessary to live in a style appropriate to their rank were only possible by waiting constantly on Louis. For this purpose, an elaborate court ritual was created where the king became the centre of attention and was observed throughout the day by the public. With his excellent memory, Louis could then see who attended him at court and who was absent, facilitating the subsequent distribution of favours and positions. Another tool Louis used to control his nobility was censorship, which often involved the opening of letters to discern their author's opinion of the government and king. Moreover, by entertaining, impressing, and domesticating them with extravagant luxury and other distractions, Louis not only cultivated public opinion of him, but also ensured the aristocracy remained under his scrutiny. Louis' extravagance at Versailles extended far beyond the scope of elaborate court rituals. In an excerpt from Diderot's Encyclopédie, Louis-Jean-Marie Daubenton recounts a story in which Louis took delivery of an African elephant as a gift.

In 1668 the king of Portugal sent an elephant from the kingdom of Congo to the king of France. It was seventeen years old and measured six and a half feet from the ground to the top of its back. The elephant lived in the menagerie at Versailles for thirteen years and only grew a further foot, no doubt because the change in climate and food had stunted its growth; so it measured just seven and a half feet when the gentlemen of the Royal Academy of Sciences carried out their description of it. This, along with the prohibition of private armies, prevented them from passing time on their own estates and in their regional power-bases, from which they historically waged local wars and plotted resistance to royal authority. Louis thus compelled and seduced the old military aristocracy (the "nobility of the sword") into becoming his ceremonial courtiers, further weakening their power. In their place, Louis raised commoners or the more recently ennobled bureaucratic aristocracy (the "nobility of the robe"). He judged that royal authority thrived more surely by filling high executive and administrative positions with these men because they could be more easily dismissed than nobles of ancient lineage with entrenched influence. It is believed that Louis's policies were rooted in his experiences during the Fronde, when men of high birth readily took up the rebel cause against their king, who was actually the kinsman of some. This victory over the nobility may have then in fact ensured the end of major civil wars in France until the French Revolution about a century later.

REVOCATION OF THE EDICT OF NANTES

It has traditionally been suggested that the devout Madame de Maintenon pushed Louis to persecute Protestants and revoke the 1598 Edict of Nantes, which awarded Huguenots political and religious freedom, but her influence in the matter is now being questioned. Louis himself saw the persistence of Protestantism as a disgraceful reminder of royal powerlessness. After all, the Edict was the pragmatic concession of his grandfather Henry IV to end the longstanding French Wars of Religion. An additional factor in Louis's thinking was the prevailing contemporary European principle to assure socio-political stability was cuius regio, eius religio *("whose realm, his religion")*, the idea that the religion of the ruler should be the religion of the realm (as originally confirmed in central Europe in the Peace of Augsburg of 1555). Responding to petitions, Louis initially excluded Protestants from office, constrained the meeting of synods, closed churches outside Edict-stipulated areas, banned Protestant outdoor preachers, and prohibited domestic Protestant migration. He also disallowed Protestant-Catholic intermarriages where third parties objected, encouraged missions to the Protestants, and rewarded converts to Catholicism. This discrimination did not encounter much Protestant resistance, and a steady conversion of Protestants occurred, especially among the noble elites. In 1681, Louis dramatically increased his persecution of Protestants. The principle of cuius regio, eius religio generally had also meant that subjects who refused to convert could emigrate, but Louis banned emigration and effectively insisted that all Protestants must be converted. Secondly, following the proposal of René de Marillac and the Marquis of Louvois, he began quartering dragoons in Protestant homes. Although this was within his legal rights, the dragonnades inflicted severe financial strain on Protestants and atrocious abuse. Between 300,000 and 400,000 Huguenots converted, as this entailed financial rewards and exemption from the

le Peuple Sous l'ancien Regime

▲ *Another satire sheet about the conditions of the third Estate.*

dragonnades. On 15 October 1685, Louis issued the Edict of Fontainebleau, which cited the redundancy of privileges for Protestants given their scarcity after the extensive conversions. The Edict of Fontainebleau revoked the Edict of Nantes, and repealed all the privileges that arose therefrom. By his edict, Louis no longer tolerated Protestant groups, pastors, or churches to exist in France. No further churches were to be constructed, and those already existing were to be demolished. Pastors could choose either exile or a secular life. Those Protestants who had resisted conversion were now to be baptised forcibly into the established church. Protestant peasants rebelled against the officially sanctioned dragonnades (conversions enforced by dragoons, labeled *"missionaries in boots"*) that followed the Edict of Fontainebleau.

Writers have debated Louis's reasons for issuing the Edict of Fontainebleau. He may have been seeking to placate Pope Innocent XI, with whom relations were tense and whose aid was necessary to determine the outcome of a succession crisis in the Electorate of Cologne. He may also have acted to upstage Emperor Leopold I and regain international prestige after the latter defeated the Turks without Louis's help. Otherwise, he may simply have desired to end the remaining divisions in French society dating to the Wars of Religion by fulfilling his coronation oath to eradicate heresy. Many historians have condemned the Edict of Fontainebleau as gravely harmful to France.

In support, they cite the emigration of about 200,000 Huguenots (roughly one-fourth of the Protestant population, or 1% of the French population) who defied royal decrees, fled France for various Protestant states, and took their skills with them. On the other hand, there are historians who view this as an exaggeration. They argue that most of France's preeminent Protestant businessmen and industrialists converted to Catholicism and remained.

What is certain is that reaction to the Edict was mixed. Even while French Catholic leaders exulted, Pope Innocent XI still argued with Louis over Gallicanism and criticised the use of violence. Protestants across Europe were horrified at the treatment of their co-religionists, but most Catholics in France applauded the move. Nonetheless, what is sure is that Louis's public image in most of Europe, especially in Protestant regions, was dealt a severe blow. In the end, however, despite renewed tensions with the Camisards of south-central France at the end of his reign, Louis may have helped ensure that his successor would experience fewer instances of the religion-based disturbances that had plagued his forebears. French society would sufficiently change by the time of his descendant Louis XVI to welcome toleration in the form of the 1787 Edict of Versailles, also known as the Edict of Tolerance. This restored to non-Catholics their civil rights and the freedom to worship openly.

LEAGUE OF AUGSBURG
Causes and conduct of the war

The War of the League of Augsburg, which lasted from 1688 to 1697, initiated a period of decline in Louis's political and diplomatic fortunes. The conflict arose from two events in the Rhineland. First, in 1685, the Elector Palatine Charles II died. All that remained of his immediate family was Louis's sister-in-law, Elizabeth Charlotte. German law ostensibly barred her from succeeding to her brother's lands and electoral dignity, but it was unclear enough for arguments in favour of Elizabeth Charlotte to have a chance of success. Conversely, the princess was quite clearly entitled to a division of the family's personal property. Louis pressed her claims to land and chattels, hoping that the latter at least would be given to her. Then, in 1688, Maximilian Henry of Bavaria, Archbishop of Cologne, an ally of France, died. The archbishopric had traditionally been held by the Wittelsbachs of Bavaria. However, the Bavarian claimant to replace Maximilian Henry, Prince Joseph Clemens of Bavaria, was at that time not more than 17 years old and not even ordained. Louis sought instead to install his own candidate, William Egon of Fürstenberg, to ensure the key Rhenish state remained an ally. In light of his foreign and domestic policies during the early 1680s, which were perceived as aggressive, Louis's actions fostered by the succession crises of the late 1680s created concern and alarm in much of Europe. This led to the formation of the 1686 League of Augsburg by the Holy Roman Emperor, Spain, Sweden, Saxony, and Bavaria. Their stated intention was to return France to at least the borders agreed to in the Treaty of Nijmegen. Emperor Leopold I's persistent refusal to convert the Truce of Ratisbon into a permanent treaty fed Louis's fears that the Emperor would turn on France and attack the Reunions after settling his affairs in the Balkans. Another event that Louis found threatening was the Glorious Revolution of 1688 in England. Although King James II was Catholic, his two Anglican daughters, Mary and Anne, ensured the English people a Protestant succession. However, when James II's son James was born, he took precedence in the succession over his elder sisters. This

▲ *Another satire sheet about the conditions of the third Estate.*

seemed to herald an era of Catholic monarchs in England. Protestant lords took up arms and called on the Dutch Prince William III of Orange, grandson of Charles I of England, to come to their aid. He sailed for England with troops despite Louis's warning that France would regard it as a provocation. Witnessing numerous desertions and defections, even among those closest to him, James II fled England.

Parliament declared the throne vacant, and offered it to James's daughter Mary II and his son-in-law and nephew William. Vehemently anti-French, William (now William III of England) pushed his new kingdoms into war, thus transforming the League of Augsburg into the Grand Alliance.

Before this happened, Louis expected William's expedition to England to absorb his energies and those of his allies, so he dispatched troops to the Rhineland after the expiry of his ultimatum to the German princes requiring confirmation of the Truce of Ratisbon and acceptance of his demands about the succession crises.

This military manoeuvre was also intended to protect his eastern provinces from Imperial invasion by depriving the enemy army of sustenance, thus explaining the pre-emptive scorched earth policy pursued in much of southwestern Germany (the *"Devastation of the Palatinate"*).

French armies were generally victorious throughout the war because of Imperial commitments in the Balkans, French logistical superiority, and the quality of French generals such as Condé's famous pupil, François Henri de Montmorency-Bouteville, duc de Luxembourg. His triumphs at the Battles of Fleurus in 1690, Steenkerque in 1692, and Landen in 1693 preserved northern France from invasion.

Although an attempt to restore James II failed at the Battle of the Boyne in 1690, France accumulated a string of victories from Flanders in the north, Germany in the east, and Italy and Spain in the south, to the high seas and the colonies. Louis personally supervised the captures of Mons in 1691 and Namur in 1692.

Luxembourg gave France the defensive line of the Sambre by capturing Charleroi in 1693. France also overran most of the Duchy of Savoy after the battles of Marsaglia and Staffarde in 1693.

While naval stalemate ensued after the French victory at the Battle of Beachy Head in 1690 and the Allied victory at Barfleur-La Hougue in 1692, the Battle of Torroella in 1694 exposed Catalonia to French invasion, culminating in the capture of Barcelona. Although the Dutch captured Pondichéry in 1693, a French raid on the Spanish treasure port of Cartagena in 1697 yielded a fortune of 10.000.000 livres. In July 1695, the city of Namur, occupied for three years by the French, was besieged by an allied army led by William III. Louis XIV ordered the surprise destruction of a Flemish city to divert the attention of these troops. This led to the bombardment of Brussels, in which 4-5000 buildings were destroyed, including the entire city-center. The strategy failed, as Namur fell three weeks later, but harmed Louis XIV's reputation: a century later, Napoleon deemed the bombardment *"as barbarous as it was useless."* Peace was broached by Sweden in 1690. And, by 1692, both sides evidently wanted peace, and secret bilateral talks began, but to no avail. Louis tried to break up the alliance against him by dealing with individual opponents, but this did not achieve its aim until 1696, when the Savoyards agreed to the Treaty of Turin and switched sides. Thereafter, members of the League of Augsburg rushed to the peace table, and negotiations for a general peace began in earnest, culminating in the Treaty of Ryswick of 1697.

TREATY OF RYSWICK

The Treaty of Ryswick ended the War of the League of Augsburg and disbanded the Grand Alliance. By manipulating their rivalries and suspicions, Louis divided his enemies and broke their power. The treaty yielded many benefits for France. Louis secured permanent French sovereignty over all of Alsace, including Strasbourg, and established the Rhine as the Franco-German border to this day. Pondichéry and Acadia were returned to France, and Louis's de facto possession of Saint-Domingue was recognised as lawful. However, he returned Catalonia and most of the Reunions. French military superiority might have allowed him to press for more advantageous terms. Thus, his generosity to Spain with regard to Catalonia has been read as a concession to foster pro-French sentiment and may ultimately have induced King Charles II to name Louis's grandson Philip, Duke of Anjou, as heir to the throne of Spain.

In exchange for financial compensation, France renounced its interests in the Electorate of Cologne and the Palatinate. Lorraine, which had been occupied by the French since 1670, was returned to its rightful Duke Leopold, albeit with a right of way to the French military. William and Mary were recognised as joint sovereigns of the British Isles, and Louis withdrew support for James II. The Dutch were given the right to garrison forts in the Spanish Netherlands that acted as a protective barrier against possible French aggression. Though in some respects, the Treaty of Ryswick may appear a diplomatic defeat for Louis since he failed to place client rulers in control of the Palatinate or the Electorate of Cologne, he did in fact fulfil many of the aims laid down in his 1688 ultimatum. In any case, peace in 1697 was desirable to Louis, since France was exhausted from the costs of the war.

WAR OF THE SPANISH SUCCESSION
Causes and build-up to the war

By the time of the Treaty of Ryswick, the Spanish succession had been a source of concern to European leaders for well over forty years. King Charles II ruled a vast empire comprising Spain, Naples, Sicily, Milan, the Spanish Netherlands, and numerous Spanish colonies. He produced no children, however, and consequently had no direct heirs. The principal claimants to the throne of Spain belonged to the ruling families of France and Austria. The French claim derived from Louis XIV's mother Anne of Austria (the older sister of Philip IV of Spain) and his wife Maria Theresa (Philip IV's eldest daughter). Based on the laws of primogeniture, France had the better claim as it originated from the eldest daughters in two generations. However, their renunciation of succession rights complicated matters. In the case of Maria Theresa, nonetheless, the renunciation was considered null and void owing to Spain's breach of her marriage contract with Louis. In contrast, no renunciations tainted the claims of the Emperor Leopold I's son Charles, Archduke of Austria, who was a grandson of Philip III's youngest daughter Maria Anna. The English and Dutch feared that a French or Austrian-born Spanish king would threaten the balance of power and thus preferred the Bavarian Prince Joseph Ferdinand, a grandson of Leopold I through his first wife Margaret Theresa of Spain (the younger daughter of Philip IV). In an attempt to avoid war, Louis signed the Treaty of the Hague with William III of England in 1698. This agreement divided Spain's Italian territories between Louis's son le Grand Dauphin and the Archduke Charles, with the rest of the empire awarded to Joseph Ferdinand. William III consented to permitting the Dauphin's new territories to become part of France when the latter succeeded to his father's throne. The signatories, however, omitted to consult the ruler of these lands, and Charles II was passionately opposed to the dismemberment of his empire. In 1699, he re-confirmed his 1693 will that named Joseph Ferdinand as his sole successor. Six months later, Joseph Ferdinand died. Therefore, in 1700, Louis and William III concluded a fresh partitioning agreement, the Treaty of London. This allocated Spain, the Low Countries, and the Spanish colonies to the Archduke. The Dauphin would receive all of Spain's Italian territories. Charles II acknowledged that his empire could only remain undivided by bequeathing it entirely to a Frenchman or an Austrian. Under pressure from his German wife, Maria Anna of Neuburg, Charles II named the Archduke Charles as his sole heir.

ACCEPTANCE OF THE WILL OF CHARLES II AND CONSEQUENCES

On his deathbed in 1700, Charles II unexpectedly changed his will. The clear demonstration of French military superiority for many decades before this time, the pro-French faction at the court of Spain, and even Pope Innocent XII convinced him that France was more likely to preserve his empire intact. He thus offered the entire empire to the Dauphin's second son Philip, Duke of Anjou, provided it remained undivided. Anjou was not in the direct line of French succession, thus his accession would not cause a Franco-Spanish union. If Anjou refused, the throne would be offered to his younger brother Charles, Duke of Berry. If the Duke of Berry declined it, it would go to the Archduke Charles, then to the distantly related House of Savoy if Charles declined it.

Louis was confronted with a difficult choice. He might agree to a partition of the Spanish possessions and avoid a general war, or accept Charles II's will and alienate much of Europe. Initially, Louis may have been inclined to abide by the partition treaties. However, the Dauphin's insistence persuaded Louis otherwise. Moreover, Louis's foreign minister, Jean-Baptiste Colbert, marquis de Torcy, pointed out that war with the Emperor would almost certainly ensue whether Louis accepted the partition treaties or Charles II's will. He emphasised that, should it come to war, William III was unlikely to stand by France since he "made a treaty to avoid war and did not intend to go to war to implement the treaty". Indeed, in the event of a war, it might be preferable to be already in control of the disputed lands. Eventually, therefore, Louis decided to accept Charles II's will. Philip, Duke of Anjou, thus became Philip V, King of Spain. Most European rulers accepted Philip as king, though some only reluctantly.

Depending on one's views of the war as inevitable or not, Louis acted reasonably or arrogantly. He confirmed that Philip V retained his French rights despite his new Spanish position. Admittedly, he may only have been hypothesising a theoretical eventuality and not attempting a Franco-Spanish union. But his actions were certainly not read as being disinterested. Moreover, Louis sent troops to the Spanish Netherlands to evict Dutch garrisons and secure Dutch recognition of Philip V. In 1701, Philip transferred the asiento (the right to supply slaves to Spanish colonies) to France, alienating English traders. As tensions mounted, Louis decided to acknowledge James Stuart, the son of James II, as king of England on the latter's death, infuriating William III. These actions enraged Britain and the Dutch Republic. With the Holy Roman Emperor and the petty German states, they formed another Grand Alliance and declared war on France in 1702. French diplomacy, however, secured Bavaria, Portugal, and Savoy as Franco-Spanish allies.

COMMENCEMENT OF FIGHTING

Even before war was officially declared, hostilities began with Imperial aggression in Italy. When finally declared, the War of the Spanish Succession would last almost until Louis's death, at great cost to him and the kingdom of France. The war began with French successes, however the joint talents of John Churchill, Duke of Marlborough, and Eugene of Savoy checked these victories and broke the myth of French invincibility.

The duo allowed the Palatinate and Austria to occupy Bavaria after their victory at the Battle of Blenheim. Maximilian II Emanuel, Elector of Bavaria, had to flee to the Spanish Netherlands. The impact of this victory won the support of Portugal and Savoy. Later, the Battle of Ramillies delivered the Low Countries up to the Allies, and the Battle of Turin forced Louis to evacuate Italy, leaving it open to Allied forces. Marlborough and Eugene of Savoy met again at the Battle of Oudenarde, which enabled them to mount an invasion of France.

Defeats, famine, and mounting debt greatly weakened France. Between 1693 and 1710, over two million people died in two famines, made worse as foraging armies seized food supplies from the villages. In his desperation, Louis XIV even ordered a disastrous invasion of the English island of Guernsey in the autumn of 1704 with the aim of raiding their successful harvest. By the winter of 1708–1709, Louis was willing to accept peace at nearly any cost.

He agreed that the entire Spanish empire should be surrendered to the Archduke Charles, and he also consented to return to the frontiers of the Peace of Westphalia, giving up all the territories he had acquired over sixty years of his reign. He could not speak for his grandson, however, and could not promise that Philip V would accept these terms. Thus, the Allies demanded that Louis single-handedly attack his own grandson to force these terms on him.

If he could not achieve this within the year, the war would resume. Louis could not accept these terms.

TURNING POINT

The final phases of the War of the Spanish Succession demonstrated that the Allies could not maintain the Archduke Charles in Spain just as surely as France could not retain the entire Spanish inheritance for King Philip V. The Allies were definitively expelled from central Spain by the Franco-Spanish victories at the Battles of Villaviciosa and Brihuega in 1710. French forces elsewhere remained obdurate despite their defeats. The Allies suffered a Pyrrhic victory at the Battle of Malplaquet with 21,000 casualties, twice that of the French. Eventually, France recovered its military pride with the decisive victory at Denain in 1712. French military successes near the end of the war took place against the

REVEIL DU TIERS ETAT.

▲ *A 1789 satire on the awakening of the third Estate.*

background of a changed political situation in Austria. In 1705, the Emperor Leopold I died. His elder son and successor, Joseph I, followed him in 1711. His heir was none other than the Archduke Charles, who secured control of all of his brother's Austrian land holdings. If the Spanish empire then fell to him, it would have resurrected a domain as vast as that of Holy Roman Emperor Charles V in the sixteenth century. To the maritime powers of Great Britain and the Dutch Republic, this would have been as undesirable as a Franco-Spanish union.

CONCLUSION OF PEACE

As a result of the fresh British perspective on the European balance of power, Anglo-French talks began that culminated in the 1713 Treaty of Utrecht between Louis, Philip V of Spain, Anne, Queen of Great Britain, and the Dutch Republic. In 1714, after losing Landau and Freiburg, the Holy Roman Emperor also made peace with France in the Treaties of Rastatt and Baden. In the general settlement, Philip V retained Spain and its colonies, whereas Austria received the Spanish Netherlands and divided Spanish Italy with Savoy. Britain kept Gibraltar and Minorca. Louis agreed to withdraw his support for James Stuart, son of James II and pretender to the throne of Great Britain, and ceded Newfoundland, Rupert's Land, and Acadia in the Americas to Anne. Britain gained most from the Treaty of Utrecht, but the final terms were much more favourable to France than what was being discussed in peace negotiations in 1709 and 1710. France retained Île-Saint-Jean and Île Royale, and Louis did acquire a few minor European territories, such as the Principality of Orange and the Ubaye Valley, which covered transalpine passes into Italy. Thanks to Louis, his allies the Electors of Bavaria and Cologne were restored to their pre-war status and returned their lands.

THE
COLOUR
PLATES

PLATES LIST OF ILLUSTRATIONS

82 Bourbon. Flag of 1725. Chasseur in 1789.

83 Beauvoiais. Flag of 1725. Sergeant of Grenadiers in 1789

84 *Rouergue. Flag Officer in 1725. in 1789.*

85 Bourgogne. Grenadier in 1789. Flag of 1725.

86 Royal-Marine. Flag of 1730. Adjutant in 1789.

87 Grenadier Vermandois in 1789 Flag of 1730

88 *Salm-Salm. Flag of 1730. Banner-Colonel in 1760. Grenadier in 1789.*

89 Royal-Artillerie. Flag of 1680. Sergeant in 1715.

90 Royal-Artillerie. Miners and gunners in 1763

91 Royal-Artillerie. Coast Canonnier and conductors wagons in 1780.

92 Royal-Artillerie. Officier in 1789. Canonnier in 1775.

93 Royal-Italien. Flag in 1720. Sergeant in 1760. Grenadier in 1788.

94 Ernest. Flag of 1730. Grenadier in 1789.

95 Salis-Samade. Flag of 1730. Grenadier in 1789.

96 Sonnemberg. Flag of 1730. Captain in 1789.

97 Castellas. Flag of 1730. Sergeant in 1789.

98 Languedoc. Flag of 1750. Chasseur in 1789.

99 Beauce. Flag of 1730. Sub-Lieutenant in 1789.

100 Vigier. Flag of 1730. Grenadier in 1789.

101 Médoc. Grenadier in 1789. Soldier and Banner in 1735.

102 *Vivarais. Sergeant in 1789. Flag of 1689.*

103 Vexin. Grenadiers of 1776 to 1795. Flag in 1700. Soldier in 1750.

104 Royal-Comtois. Flag of 1730. Rifleman in 1789.

105 Beaujolais. Soldier in 1750. Officier in 1776 and 1789.

106 Monsieur. Official Flag Officer in 1725. 1775. 1789

107 Chateauvieux. Flag of 1750. Grenadier in 1789.

108 The Mark. Grenadier in 1789. Flag in 1720.

109 Penthièvre. Official in 1789. Standard bearer 1776.

110 Boulonnais-Angoumois. Flag in 1720. Soldier in 1789

111 *Saintonge Officier in 1789. Flag in 1715 Conti Chasseur in 1789.*

112 Rohan. Grenadier in 1789 Foix. Flag in 1725 Chasseur in 1789.

113 Diesbach. Chasseur in 1789. Flag of the 1730

114 *Courlen Sergeant in 1789. Flag of 1725.*

115 *Dillon. Soldier in 1789. Flag of 1740*

116 Berwick. Officier in 1789. Flag of 1745.

117 Royal-Suédois. Standard bearer 1789. Sergeant in 1715.

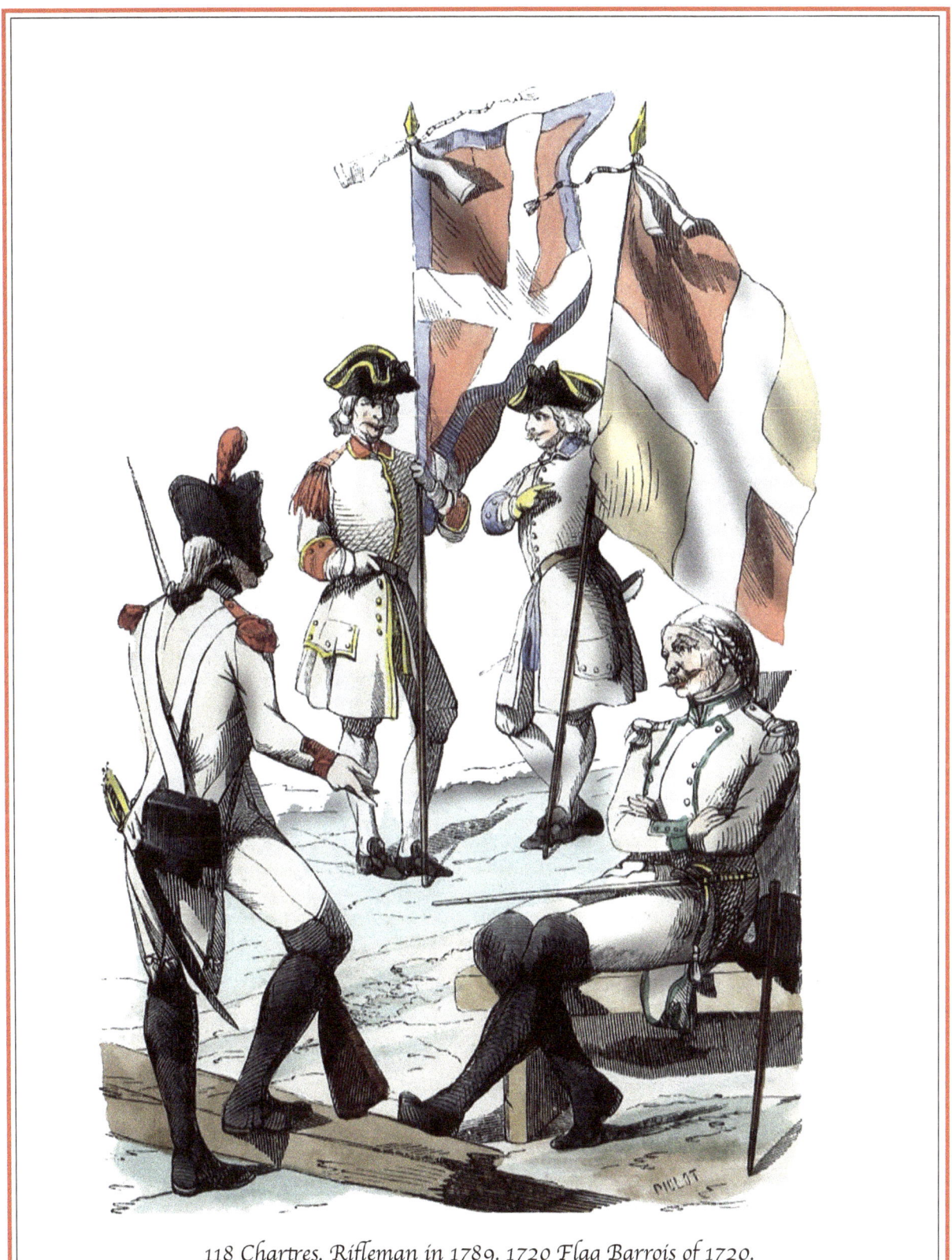

118 Chartres. Rifleman in 1789. 1720 Flag Barrois of 1720.

119 Walsh. Flag of 1715. Soldier in 1776 and 1789.

120 Enghien. Corporal in 1789. 1706 Flag Corporal in 1776.

121 Royal-Hesse-Darmstadt. Flag of 1720. Grenadier in 1789.

122 provincial troops. Royal Grenadiers of Picardie, the Normandie, dell'Orleanais and Bretagne

123 Salis-Marschlins. Drum in 1765. Rifleman of 1734. Flag in 1789.

124 Royal-Corse. Soldier in 1739. Standard bearer 1788

125 Nassau. Chasseur in 1789. Flag of 1745

126 Steiner Officer in 1789. Flag in 1752.

127 Bouillon. Officier in 1757. Standard bearer 1789

128 Royal-Deux-Ponts. Grenadier and Banner in 1789. Sergeant in 1757.

129 Reinach, Rifleman in 1789. 1758 Flag.

130 Montréal. Soldier in 1786. Royal-Liégeois. Standard bearer 1789.

131 Troops read. Chasseurs des Alpes, the Cevennes and the Ardennes in 1787.

132 colonial troops in 1789. Pondicherry. Grenadier, La Martinique. Chasseur. Le Cap. Drum.

133 Nice in 1750. Berry in 1760. Cambis in 1760.

134 *La Marche in 1760. Hainaut in 1760. Forez in 1770*

135 Beauce in 1748. Nivernais in 1760. Isle-de-Franee in 1760

136 Luxembourg in 1748. Beaujolais in 1748. Fleury in 1748.

137 *La Tour d'Auvergne in 1748. Gatinais in 1748. Blesois in 1748.*

138 Auxerrois in 1748. Landes in 1748. Agénois in 1748.

139 Harquebusier of Grassin in 1748. Lowendhal in 1760. Hallweyl in 1760.

140 Royal-Lorraine in 1750. Royal-Wallon in 1748. Royal-Ecossaises in 1755.

141 Lally in 1755. The Rifleman de Morliere in 1748. Royal-Cantabre in 1748.

142 Royal-Pologne in 1755. Saint-Germain in 1755. Volunteer Breton in 1748.

143 Volunteer, Wurmser in 1762. Volunteer Dauphiné in 1760. Vierzet in 1760.

144 Légion de Hainaut in 1763. Legion races in 1769. Légion de Flandre in 1763

145 Légion royale in 1775. Légion de Condé in 1775. Infanterie de Marine in 1772.

146 Légion de Soubise in 1775. Légion de Dauphiné in 1775. Provincial races in 1786.

147 Invalid in 1789. Canonnière retired in 1789. Official French retired in 1789.

148 Swiss German retired in 1789. Retired in 1789. Irish retired in 1789.

149 Maréchal de camp (small seal). Lieutenant - General and Aide de camp in 1789.

150 Engineer geographer engineer officer in 1789. Lieutenant du Roi.

151 Army Medical. regimental surgeon in 1789. Commissaire des Guerres.

COLOUR
PLATES
APPENDIX

152 Rifleman of Morliere 1745

153 French Guard 1756

154 Maison du Roi - Garde de la Porte 1750

155 Rifleman and Grenadier Regiment Provence 1750

156 Guardia de la Prevote Hotel du Roi 1750

157 Dragoons Regiment of Saxony in 1762 and regimental colonel-general in 1725

158 Maison du Roi Garde du Corps to Gendarme de la Garde 1730

159 *Brigadier Musketeers first company in 1725*

160 Harquebusier and captain of the gendarmes of France in 1610

T. I, p. 176.

Typ. Ernest Meyer, à Paris.

161 *Irish Regiments: Clare, Dillon, Lally and Roth 1750*

162 Horion (Liege) and Royal Pologne 1757

163 Royal Scots and Royal Swedish 1757

SOLDIERS, WEAPONS & UNIFORMS ALREADY PUBLISHED
(SOME TITLES)

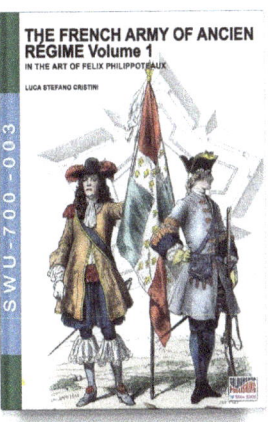

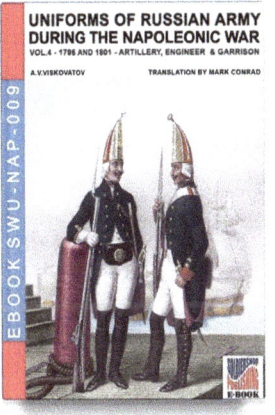

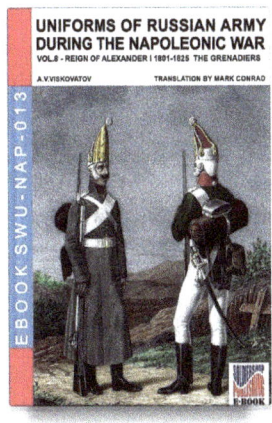